# HUMMINGBIRD

David M. Schwartz is an award-winning author of children's books, on a wide variety of topics, loved by children around the world. Dwight Kuhn's scientific expertise and artful eye work together with the camera to capture the awesome wonder of the natural world.

**Please visit our web site at: www.garethstevens.com**
**For a free color catalog describing Gareth Stevens Publishing's list of high-quality books**
**and multimedia programs, call 1-800-542-2595 (USA) or 1-800-461-9120 (Canada).**
**Gareth Stevens Publishing's Fax: (414) 332-3567.**

**Library of Congress Cataloging-in-Publication Data**

Schwartz, David M.
    Hummingbird / by David M. Schwartz; photographs by Dwight Kuhn. — North American ed.
       p. cm. — (Life cycles: a springboards into science series)
    Includes bibliographical references and index.
    ISBN 0-8368-2975-1 (lib. bdg.)
    1. Hummingbirds—Life cycles—Juvenile literature. [1. Hummingbirds.] I. Kuhn, Dwight, ill.
  II. Title.
  QL696.A558S38   2001
  598.7'64—dc21                         2001031460

This North American edition first published in 2001 by
**Gareth Stevens Publishing**
A World Almanac Education Group Company
330 West Olive Street, Suite 100
Milwaukee, WI 53212 USA

First published in the United States in 1999 by Creative Teaching Press, Inc., P.O. Box 2723, Huntington Beach, CA 92647-0723.
Text © 1999 by David M. Schwartz; photographs © 1999 by Dwight Kuhn. Additional end matter © 2001 by Gareth Stevens, Inc.

Gareth Stevens editor: Mary Dykstra

Printed in the United States of America

1 2 3 4 5 6 7 8 9 05 04 03 02 01

# HUMMINGBIRD

by David M. Schwartz
photographs by Dwight Kuhn

A SPRINGBOARDS INTO
**SCIENCE**
S E R I E S

Gareth Stevens Publishing
A WORLD ALMANAC EDUCATION GROUP COMPANY

With a loud hum and a flash of green, a tiny bird zips from flower to flower. Its wings are a blur. The bird stops in midair and hovers in place. Its feathers gleam and seem to change color in the sunlight. It is a hummingbird, the world's smallest bird.

A hummingbird's nest is a tiny cup about the size of a walnut shell. Nothing bigger than a penny can fit inside! A female hummingbird builds the nest by herself out of spider silk and small pieces of plants.

When her nest is ready, the female looks for a mate. She chooses a male, and the two birds mate in midair. Then the female goes back to her nest.

A female hummingbird will lay one or two tiny eggs. Each egg is the size of a raisin. Hummingbird eggs are the smallest eggs in the world. Next to a hummingbird's egg, a chicken's egg is huge!

A mother hummingbird sits on her eggs for two to three weeks, keeping them warm. Then the eggs hatch.

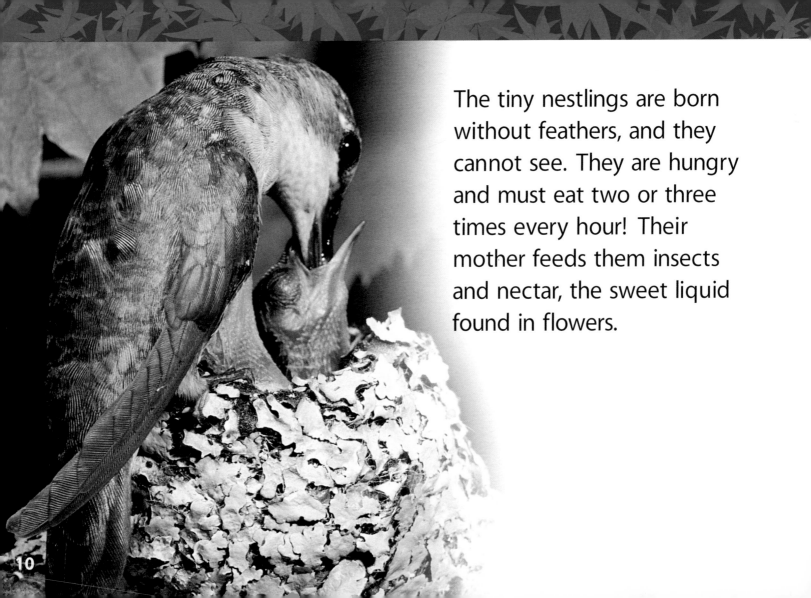

The tiny nestlings are born without feathers, and they cannot see. They are hungry and must eat two or three times every hour! Their mother feeds them insects and nectar, the sweet liquid found in flowers.

Baby hummingbirds stay in the nest for about three weeks. During this time, they open their eyes, and they begin to grow feathers.

When young hummingbirds are ready to fly, they fledge and leave the nest. Now they are called fledglings. Their feathers are a dull color so predators will not notice them. On a fledgling's first few flights, it might fall to the ground. But it always tries again and soon becomes a skilled flier.

A hummingbird can fly forward, backward, and sideways, and it can hover in place like a helicopter. This tiny bird can beat its wings as many as 80 times in one second! Because the wings are beating so fast, they make a humming sound, which is why this bird is called a hummingbird.

For hummingbirds, a flower is like a candy store. The candy is sugary nectar. It is full of energy. To get the nectar, a hummingbird pokes its long, thin beak deep inside the flower. Then it flicks its long tongue, lapping nectar the way a kitten laps milk. While drinking nectar, a hummingbird can flick its tongue 13 times in one second!

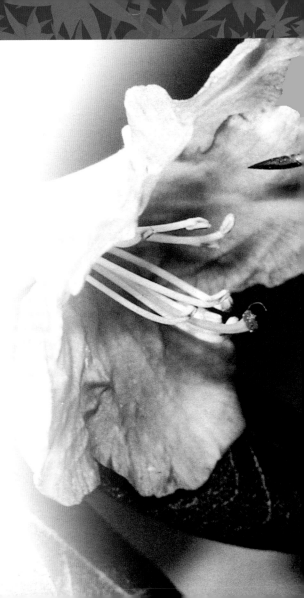

Hummingbirds also drink sugary water that people put in feeders. Hummingbird feeders are often red because red is the color of many flowers that are rich with nectar.

This male hummingbird has stopped to rest on a branch, but he will not stay there very long. Perhaps he will fly off to find a mate. Then a new generation of tiny hummingbirds will be born.

Can you put these steps in the life cycle of a hummingbird in order?

**Answer**

**blur:** a sight that is fuzzy, or not clear, often because an object is moving very fast.

**fledge:** grow feathers for flying.

**flicks:** makes quick, light movements, often with only the tip of an object, such as a finger.

**generation:** all of the young that are born during a particular time period.

**gleam** *(v)*: show short, bright flashes of light.

**hatch:** break open.

**hovers:** hangs in midair without moving up, down, or sideways in any direction.

**lapping:** drinking by dipping with the tip of the tongue and flicking liquid into the mouth.

**mate** *(n)*: either the male or female in a pair of animals that come together to produce young; *(v)* join male and female cells together to produce young.

**nestlings:** young birds that have not left the nest or started to fly.

**pokes:** pushes forward or jabs, usually with a pointed object.

**predators:** animals that hunt other animals for food.

**skilled:** very good at performing an activity that usually requires special training and practice to learn.

**spider silk:** the fine threads produced by a spider and used to build its web.

# ACTIVITIES

## Home, Sweet Home

Birds' nests can be many shapes and sizes, from the tiny nests of hummingbirds to the huge stick nests made by hawks and eagles. Go for a walk in a forest or a park or at a nature center and look for nests. Try to guess what kind of bird made each nest. A library will have books that show pictures of different nests and describe the materials birds use to make them.

## The Same, But Different

Look carefully at the pictures in this book. Do all the hummingbirds look alike? Using library books and web sites on the Internet, try to find information about different species, or kinds, of hummingbirds. How many varieties of these tiny birds can you find? In what ways are the species different from each other? In what ways are all hummingbirds alike?

## Sweet Treat

Mix up some "nectar" in your own kitchen. Stir together 1 cup (200 grams) of sugar and 4 cups (1 liter) of water. Ask an adult to boil the mixture on the stove or in a microwave, then place it in the refrigerator. When your "nectar" is cool, carefully fill a hummingbird feeder with it and hang the feeder in your backyard. Then watch for thirsty hummingbirds to stop for a treat.

## Take a Peak at Beaks

You can sometimes tell what a bird eats by looking at the size and shape of its beak. A hummingbird's long, thin beak is perfect for drinking nectar from flowers, but it wouldn't work well for cracking open seeds. Look at different beaks in a bird book. Try to guess what each kind of bird eats, just by looking at its beak.

## More Books to Read

*Animals and Their Eggs. Animals Up Close (series).* Renne (Gareth Stevens)
*Baby Birds: Growing and Flying. Secrets of the Animal World (series).* Eulalia Garcia (Gareth Stevens)
*Hummingbirds. Backyard Birds (series).* Lynn M. Stone (Rourke)
*A Hummingbird's Life. Nature Upclose (series).* John Himmelman (Children's Press)
*Little Green.* Keith Baker (Harcourt Brace)
*Ruby-Throated Hummingbirds.* James E. Gerholdt (Abdo & Daughters)

## Videos

*Baby Birds.* (Wood Knapp)
*The Hummingbird.* (Phoenix/BFA)
*Hummingbirds Up Close.* (Library Video)

## Web Sites

www.indiana.edu/~eric_rec/fl/pcto/humming.html
www.portalproductions.com/h/
www.rubythroat.org

Some web sites stay current longer than others. For additional web sites, use a good search engine to locate the following topics: *baby birds, bird feeders, hummingbirds,* and *nests.*

# INDEX